Cat Food

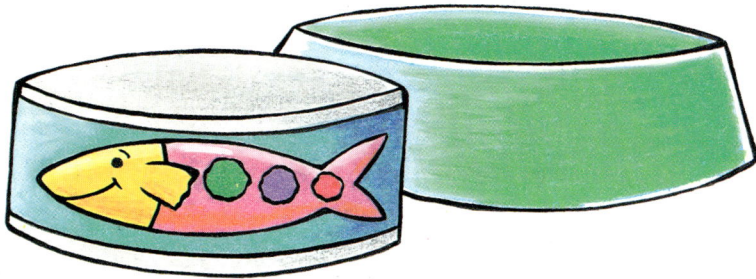

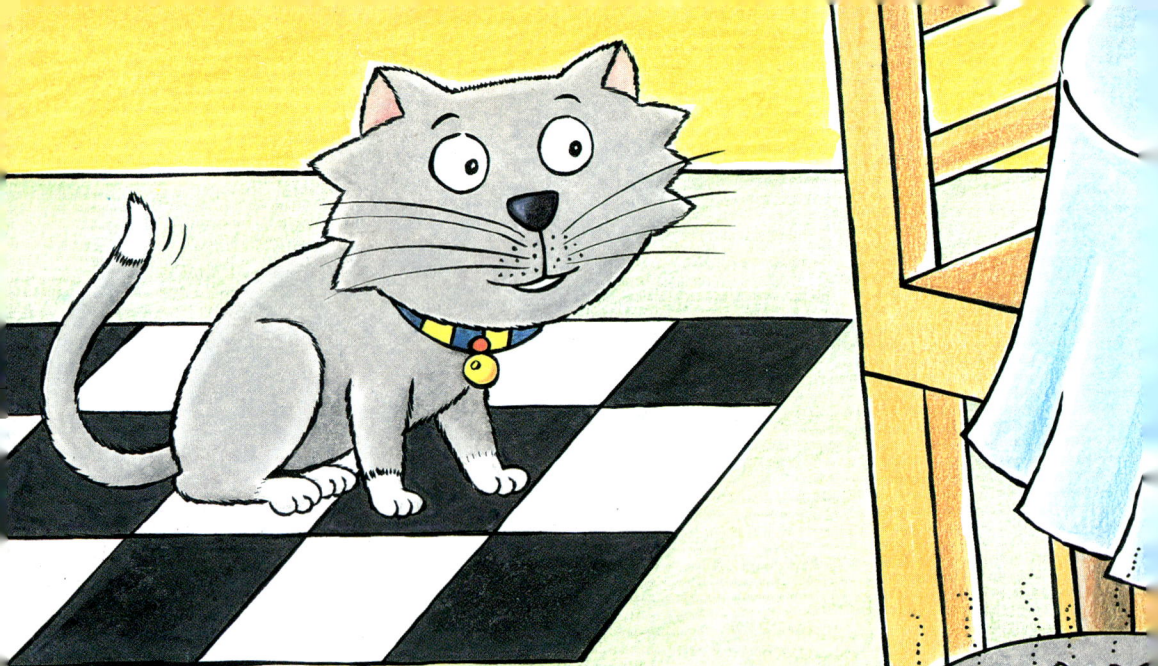

"Meow," said Kitty.
"I want my dinner."

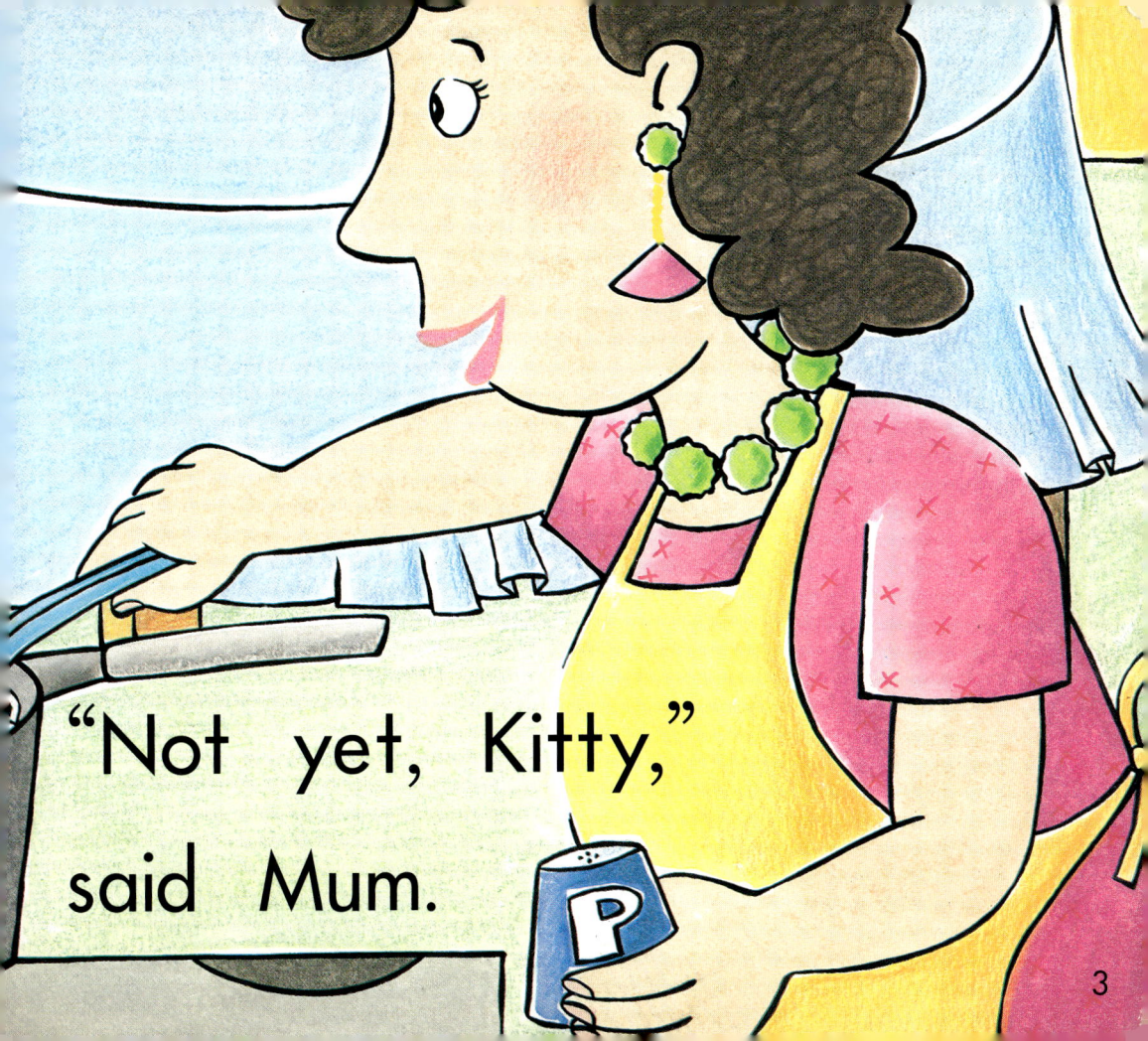

"Not yet, Kitty," said Mum.

3

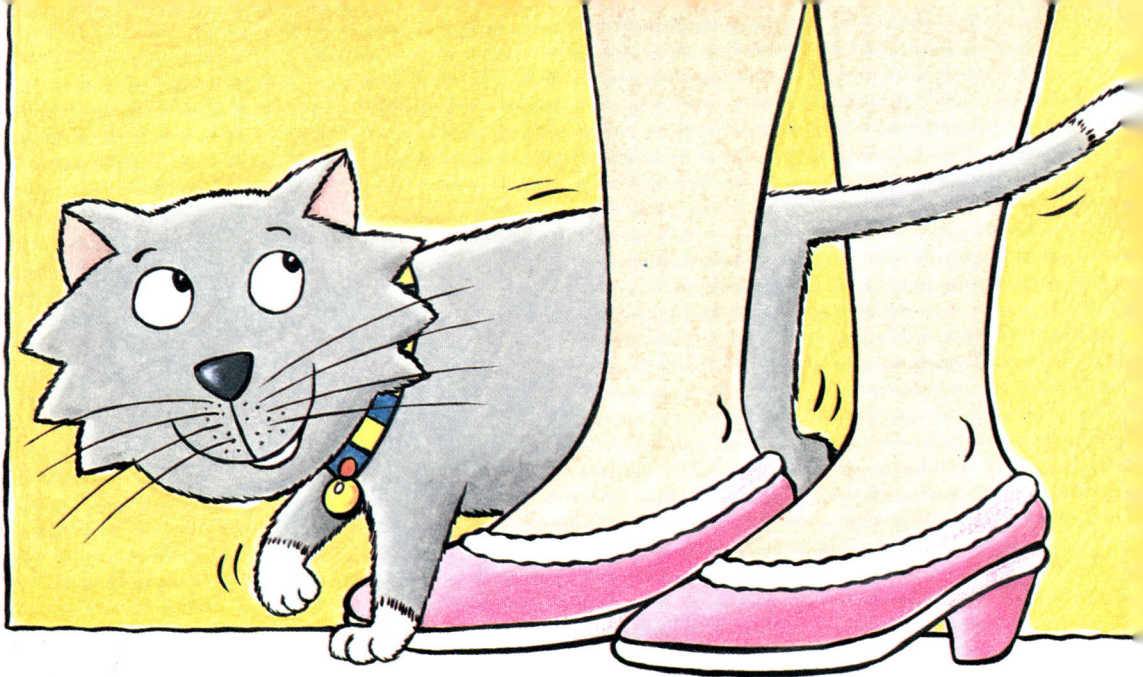

"Meow," said Kitty.

"I want my dinner."

4

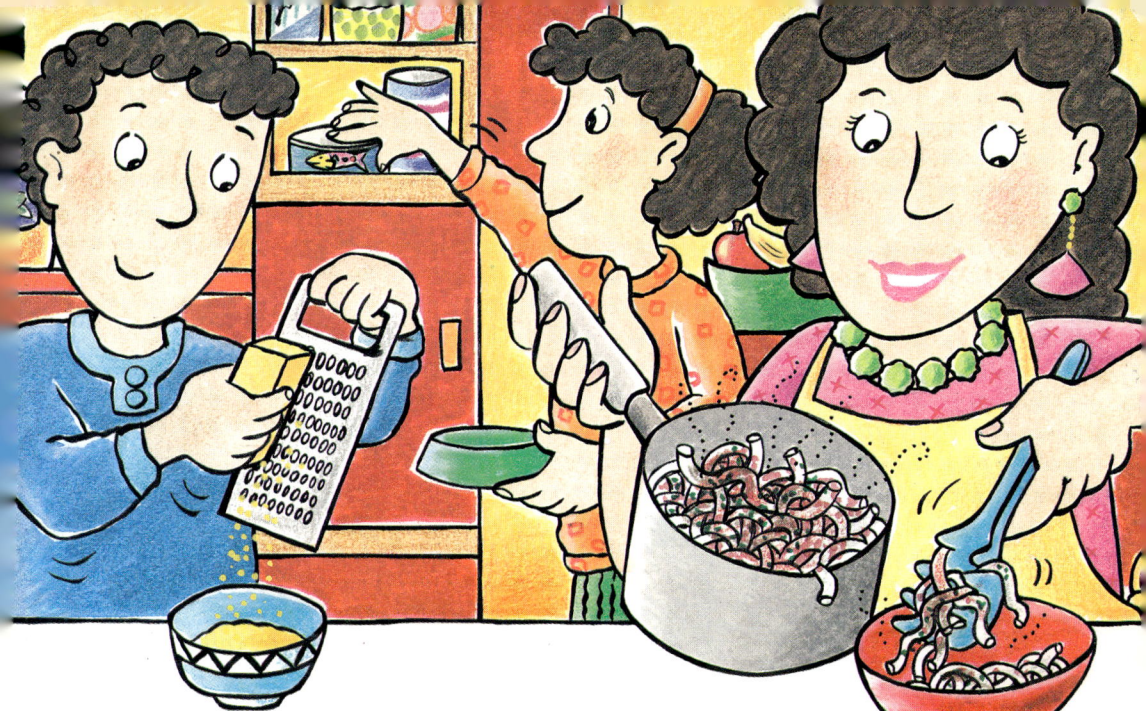

"Not yet, Kitty,"
said Mum.

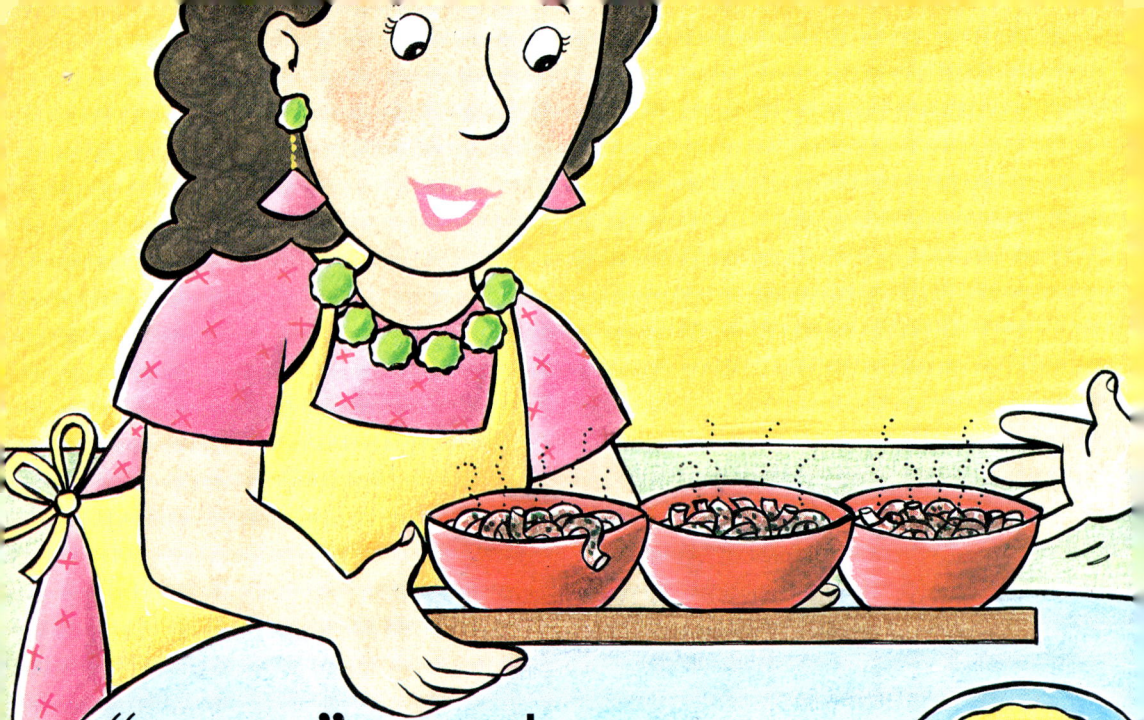

"Now," said Mum,
"let's *all* have dinner."

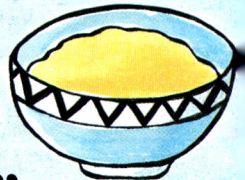

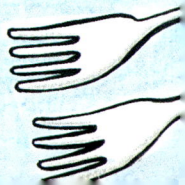

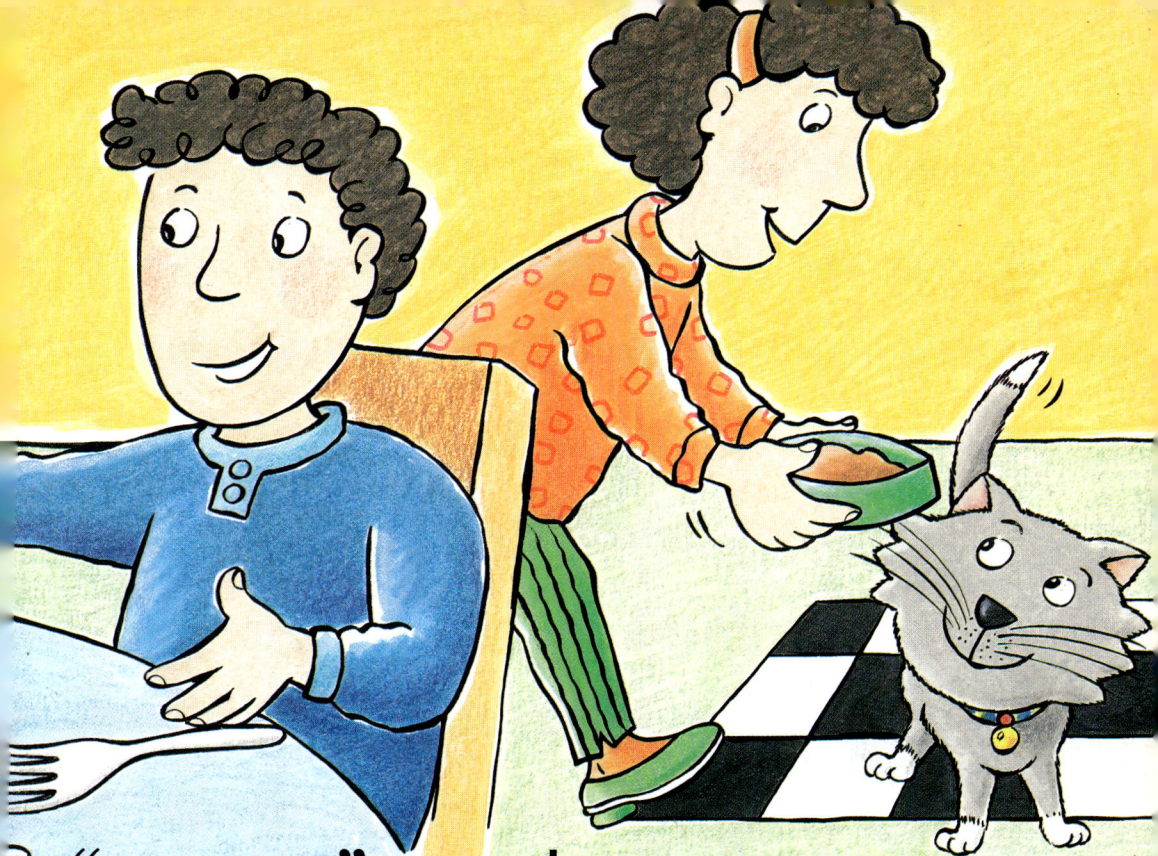

"Meow," said Kitty...

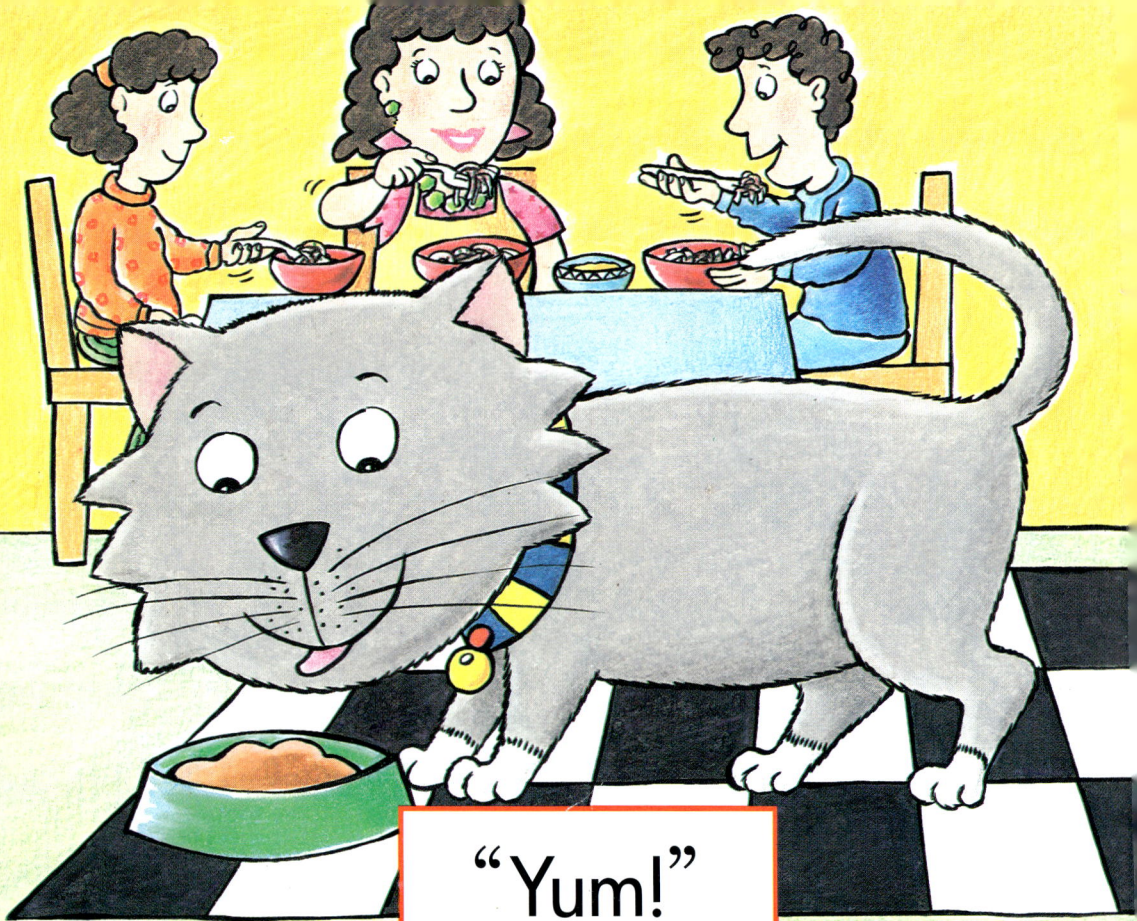

"Yum!"